Valley Therapy

By: Emanuelle Cartagena

Printed in the United States of America

FIRST EDITION

ISBN: 978-1-952352-30-0

Published by:

Crave Press

www.cravepress.com

Poems:

Valley Therapy

I am the mountain and the valley,
but the mountain is of prominence.
with its soaring peaks and glistening snowcaps.
Valleys have their own beauty,
placid meadows and blooming flowers.
But if I fall in them too deep,
I'll have trouble even seeing
the foot of the alp I wish to be.

It took me decades of falls,
3 DUIs, and years of therapy...
continuous, brisk breezes,
same words, same register, on repeat
to understand this urgent message.
But I've found the cables
to help pull me toward my whole,
the towering horn I can truly be.

A work in progress, pains and joys,
ups and downs, blend together with time.
Life's contract no one can avoid.
I can evade eternal valleys.
Make the majestic mountains
dominant in my landscape.
Pulling me up faster
when valley floods rush in.

Soul

That sugar smile, that cherry tree
The bright sunshine, the fresh mowed lawn
It all felt so good to me.

Those tall storm clouds, that nasty frown
The wilted rose, the dried up dirt
I can make it all look bad.

I'm broken and stuck. I'm rusty.
I'm just a fossil now. And I see
All the darkness and I make friends
With it as I turn to dust.

I'm laughing and one. I'm shiny new.
I'm a baby born, opening eyes
With a cry for life, and a cry for
What's coming to...

This grim but lightened soul.
Baby wails don't save
But they signal rebirth.

Or a genesis, a fusion,
Of me becoming
The sum of all my parts.

Wave Goodbye

we all wave goodbye to the past.
we talk about symptoms and solutions
as the ice caps keep meltin
and the bears and seals keep dying
the fresh suits come down on
the ladders from their private jets

we all wave goodbye to the present
they sell to the highest bidder
their fossil fuels and burning forests
while pointing their legal papers at us

we all wave goodbye to the future
as the next generation's activists
get lost in the drugs, their phones,
their parentless childhoods,
and the aimless misinformation,
"they" spread to all within earshot.

we throw their papers back at em
stand in unison, waiting their next move
They have many left. We do too.
Past, present, future collective
we ain't waving goodbye
anytime soon.

Caboose

Breath heavy, incline sharpening,
tall wheat stems blurring,
        white blind spot, sun?
Space! I've found the maze exit.

Uneven grass splotches, garages hovering
past memories of long rides circling
Stilled for years, trains rust, weeds grow.
It spoke to me. It all spoke to me.

Tiptoeing in a crimson red caboose,
bars shook upon trembling hands clutching.
Moldered leather crumbled like paper.
Particles released with each step.
Despite nearly choking, refreshing it was,
nearly folded into seat, I'm freeing, leaping

        Into a different, simple world.
        Honest, calm, voices long ago echoed,
        explaining their day's work
        unfolding family event plans
        debating their favorite songs and films.

Back into the maze I must,
to get back home but,
one last gaze reminds me,
generational gaps
maybe aren't gaps at all.

Dungeon

Amidst numerous piles of ruin
one stone structure stood, lonesome, cold, but sturdy.
        Tens to a couple hundred meet to congregate
Creaking open was a crimson red door
and slipping through was the darkness
spilling out into the rays of the bright fall day.
        "This place stays dark even in the rays of the sun.
        We meet to memorialize our fallen heroes
        of even further pasts. We celebrate their lives
        and ours that still go on."
The dungeon roared with echoes
once voice slipped through the stout stone walls.
The door never closed until you stepped in.
        "Do not close the door! The ghosts of comrades long lost
        dwell here, rest here. They allow voyeurs outside though."

Then you felt its wrath.
It'd noise drip you, gust you down,
        "One got in! Don't let the door..."
Shake you up, throw you around,
shuffle images baked in the shadows,
possible zombies or specters
and when you neared breakdown,
only then did the creaky red door re-open.
        Mass sets of eyes set in shock as they witness
        the unlucky soul who accidentally barricaded
        himself in. He was released.
        "The door just opened! He's set free!"
Bloodshot eyes, scratched face,
shaking limbs, and stuttering lips,
unfortunate he was, he may not have been.
Words of sharpness, purpose ran down,
from the transformed soul.
        "For all within earshot, hear my words!
        Spirits are meant to be held here, to rest.
        Not to be bothered! If you disturb,
        You will suffer a worse fate then me.
        Accident or not. Leave them be! Please!"

Spooked onlookers slowly backed away
while this refreshed spirit limped
further into the fading afternoon light.

DUI

Body wracked with stress, constant loop of care for all but me.
Newfound parenthood, in my first chapter of love, both
draining me to empty, little familial support,
Mate ill in many ways, escape feels like survival now.

Ah, yes, the bar, healthy release oncoming. Drive there too.
A nod to the barman, a friend, and he gets me drink one.
We catch up, he plays old loved songs, hands me three more, I'm
Dancing on counters, hugging strangers, yelling dumb facts, in time.
Then I head to two more bars to multiply the action.
In between, a quick cig pit stop, hadn't done that in five years.
At the last bar, old friend showed up, with a look I can't erase.
That, "oh shit!" look. But closing time's here, I'm okay to drive.

Stumble and slip into the seat, grip the wheel, fade to black.
Ca-boom, cr-cr-rank, crap, my car won't start. Are those cop lights?
He sees me, lights out, in the middle of the road,
After the firm knock on my window, many questions:
How many have you had? Can you walk straight? Why're your lights out?
Failed all those tests miserably. Handcuffs lock on next, in the back
(you go), Vision blurs as does the ride. Post blood test, they
Throw me on a cold holding cell bench, waiting for bail money.

My ride, my aunt, tries with words and tone, in vain, to break my tears.
Verity crushed down more witnessing my parking spot bare.
I'm a dad now. No excuses. Plus I knew what was next:
Fines, hearings, rehab, suspensions; I've done this all prior.
I just couldn't (handle to) bear another damn DUI.
Even more so the biggest price, my self-worth, my sense of self.
Already scarce and warped, it's plunging to new, scary lows.
I'm ready to dive deepest, hit the final rock bottom.

I found the steepest local cliff, weapon in hand.
I yell to myself, "I have the gun!" Earth whispers back,
"Jumping is more fun." Listening, I splash out forward,
Into the dry, warm air, falling never felt so free.

Air gusts wrap around my feet, bird chirps brush my ears.
Jet exhausts zip by, shaking space. Feel so free.
Free as...being smacked, head first into a whipping plane.
Blood splashed on the glass, carcass dangling on a wing.

Myself, dropping my poisoned guts to depths below.
Spreading wings of renewal, soaring to the sun
Of my own, the one we all have inside of us.

Cops

I feel my heartbeat, skip, race, jump,
        Empty Dominos parking lot,
        except for a lone vehicle,
        the most recognizable kind
The blue and black, the white and silver,
        They come in all different colors,
Shapes too: square-like SUVs,
oblong chevy caprice,
cut-off rectangle pickups.
I'm talking about cops. Cop cars!
I hate them. It's not their fault.
I have three DUIs on my record.
Most recent, two and a half years prior.

Tire hit, flew up, busted liner
one shredded battery wire later
Lights were out, highway stop
beer breath, oh the memories.

That night, was my own doing.
Exit home was a quarter mile ahead.
Oh, the irony. Oh, the agony!
Penance of this sin
doesn't lighten the weight of it,
something I feel each time
I see a cop car near/on a road.

Guilt of self-infliction
doesn't lighten the weight of it all,
something I feel each time
I see a cop car near/on a road.

Heaven's Bridge

A north breeze roars over a swaying bridge, crisp waters,
and an ashen gate. Sun cracks through thick clouds hovering.
Metal rattles, calls me to heaven's path, carrying great weight.
Jog, walk, slide, I'll make it there if I have to crawl. Next stride,
foot slips through cracked slat, lift up, level, and inch forward. I hear
jingles of past memories sing. Current woe doesn't deter.
Balance of mind I find with...latch reached, popped up, door opens.
Creaks aplenty, I inch front, lights warming me. I rise, live!

Tank empty, body keels over on its side. Clouds cloak the sun,
once streaking. Limbs loosen then stiffen, canceling both out.
Freezing dead, my thoughts, feels, morals all burn off life's map
and blur to grey in depths unseen. Mouth pours screams but
with no sound, no one to hear. No angel lift, rot sets in
as the gate smacks my corpse on repeat with each cold gust.

Nature Signals

Fleeting the hum of a mockingbird,
as was the buzzing of bumblebees,
capturing the last vestiges
of savoring the moment,
I propelled my personal wounds to the air.
Replete with vitriol and nectar,
I summoned my demons to my face,
and nose, caressing their delicate shadows,
fondling the bruises they inflicted.
I embraced transposing myself.
Necessary it was for me
to wear my scars as badges of honor,
and not leave them for blackmail,
or shame or humiliation.

But the bees would buzz,
and the birds hum anyway,
whether I captured myself or not.
I am not important to them.
I am to me now.
Just like nature,
I move on.

Clouds

Sharp wind, unwind, storm green coats the sky high,
unfolding foam from the top of the sea.
Rough gales batter rickety barn doors loose.
Livestock run blind, tools blow, scatter below.
Sea congealed into a thick wall; creeps close.
Branches fall, trees sway, wood crackling
rumbling like the water nearing shore.
Whitecaps crash into all, burying them.

Energy, currents, minerals, atoms,
don't immediately break down. They bounce,
diffuse, ride through the expanse, ascend far,
taking us all into space, dark matter.
Ever painted on life's picture, we are
through time, big bangs. Nirvana is science.

Together Again

Upon first sight, your orchid beauty
flashed me frozen, stunned almost silent.
Radiance of tone, elegance of gesture
splashed my face with composure
as your cries about an ex stalking
poured out of your delicate mouth.
My listening drew you in.
While we exchange numbers,
I'm happier that smile cracked through.

Honey wipe those tears from your eyes.
There's a life worth living and loving
and we can make that happen together.

Splendor of our first sleep conjoined,
thins as you rise the morning after.
All I want to do is hold you here,
laying in our fluids, vining our bodies
stitching our souls to one.
Work, student debt, medical bills
lifts you, staunchly opposed to my
wandering nothingness of no credit,
no debt, few bills, little obligation.

You wiped the tears from my eyes.
We both know there's a life worth living,
Loving together, as my tears dry.

Tumbling, fumbling, I'm waiting,
for you to make us Facebook official.
But you won't commit to that.
Ex is still out there, people gossip.
Will it put too much pressure on us?
Excuses, I say, we're knowing each other
more and more each day, why fear?
This is part of piling knowledge.
You'll find out things you don't want to.

Honey expunge those fears from your heart.
There's a life worth living and loving and
we can still make that happen together.

Unhealed from my own past,
jealousy unleashes, thinking you're flirting
at a local watering hole.
Both drunk, both cursing, you raising hands,
the waiting cab driver intervenes.
Only one gets in the vehicle,
beginning the breakup/makeup cycle,
which repeats until we run out of rebounds.

But, babe wipe those tears from your eyes.
Again, the list of agains is growing.
Together is still together. We're still...

In a couple's counseling session realizing we're
suppressing then exploding our feelings
until we burn out and grow numb to it all.
Surveying the damage wrought,
Therapy can't help heal these wounds.
We've ruined the scar tissue.

Honey wipe those tears, we're not meant to be,
timing off, I still care for you. If I can't
hold you now, maybe we'll connect again.

Reuniting at a barbecue
Friends at each other's weddings
In heaven where love lives eternal

Barren Hill

A poet, for sure,
My inner cynic?
Flees like me in stress.
Flight or fight, I fly.
Fly away from my darkest
bowels of thoughts and dreams.
When I write, I want
to look shiny, pretty
for all. But reality
is much more complex.

Truth is, large, jagged rocks
in my mind, the dim feels
come tumbling down fast
when I'm worn the hell out
and outside forces boss up.
Try stopping a rolling stone.
The decline exerts full speed
and squashes most on impact.
I let the dark thoughts fall with myself,
reach the foot, ease to a stall.
I cradle them, kiss their cuts
and embrace them like mothers
do children. They're my own.
Overstayed welcome, it's time,
you'd think, to part. It's not.
If these boulders leave my hill
will it be barren?
If I lose these thoughts
than who, really, am I?

Dad

You're there, blank face,
nearly drooling, as she screams
the agony and the intensity
of childbirth. You fall to the floor
in a moment, stumble up to sit.
mumble a second, and soon leave.
Half-drunk, you showed up for mine,
I can't say the same for my sisters.

The last time I saw you,
was kind of like the first.
Only you had that weird woman
with you. Your on again-off again lover.
Thanksgiving, little thanks, no hugs,
tired eyes, slight booze scent, and
an acknowledgement you arrived
like you deserved a medal for it.

Best $50 I ever spent, ancestry search.
Found your grave, pissed on it.
Your atonement for leaving your three kids
with an unstable mom. Like that pee,
I let go of your memories:
The few times you did show up,
and all the times you didn't.

I forgive you now, and myself
for not forgiving you sooner.
My triptych of moments with you
won't follow me like a craving lush.
It'll just float above, drift, harmless,
reminding me not to drift like you did.

Dad 2

love you,
free guilt, float free,
man up, grow up, live in
heaven like you didn't in life.
for me.

Mom

Love you,
no blame, your pick,
had warning labels. your
trauma didn’t, I forgive. live,
for me.

Parents

both housed,
demons, hurt me,
mine exposed why. I bear,
yours, your love, you, and wish to end
our pain.

When My Therapist Told Me She Wasn't Worried About Me

its time to worry
you said you don't.
I don't want you to.

shift of mind,
so abrupt,
like williwaws.
can't ever predict
when they'll turn.
why are the thaws
so slow?
why do the winds
take so long
to calm?
and so quickly
come back?
i'm sick and tired
of answering
these questions.

its time to worry.
you said you don't.
I don't want you to.
willingness,
you've used that word
with me plenty.
they say it with
addiction too,
of which a word
I've used to
describe my
consistently dark,
cynically negative
thought processes.
but no one would
say it to a Magellan
sailor who got caught
in a high, cold tide,
drowning or
succumbing to
hypothermia.
no one would say

he had no willingness
or that he was an addict.

it's time to worry
AGAIN, implying,
its just another wave.
I'll pull through it.
but you could say
that to a mountain hiker,
knowing a curt snow
could bury them.
or a savanna farmer
where any drought could
wilt their crops,
their vital life resource.

It's time to worry.
deep down, I
really want you to.
not because I'm that sick
or selfish that I'd
want you to hurt to.
but because I
never learned how
to love or form
friendships without
trauma bonding.
I think your worry
will keep you around
because I am
not loveable, normal,
being who I really am.
I'm only worthy
of love if I'm in pain.
If I'm capsizing
in the strait of Magellan
or suffocating in
Rocky mountain blizzards
or starving in African
savanna drought.

when I say
it's time to worry
this is what I

really mean.
I haven't learned
to be me yet
without realizing
pain isn't what
makes me me.
I hope you can stay
long enough for me
to figure me out.
and hopefully you
don't worry too much.
I guess that's
a bit on me to not
give you a reason
to worry.
to stay away
from the high tides,
blizzards, and droughts
in my head.

Creepy Old Man

I’d never met you before.
What were you doing in my mom's bedroom?
I was just watching TV
Why were you rubbing my back?
I was just watching TV
Why'd you go to the downstairs bathroom?
I was just watching TV
Why'd you not leave seeing my sister in there?
I was just watching TV
Why'd you stay in there with her?
I was just watching TV
Because you asked me to come downstairs
I was just watching TV
Because you asked me a bunch of other weird questions

I was just watching TV
Because there were many others getting lit
Telling their adult stories, even to my face.
Sometimes violent, even to my face,
When I "hung out" with them prior.
I was just watching TV
Because my mom was always one of the
"Sometimes violent, getting lit" adults.
But you didn't want to bring me downstairs
For all of that. No. Because if so you'd have
Lured my sisters down to "hang out".
Nah, you wanted us for yourself you sick freak.
Typical middle aged, weird vibed,
soft spoken abuser of children.

When that head of household
"sometimes violent, getting lit" adult
Was informed, no cops were called.
No investigations opened.
No hugs of comfort given.
You got to roam free afterwards.
She did brag about how
she told your nephew
Never to bring you around again.
Yay mom! She really took care of that.
Her threats must've got to you somehow.
Your presence never showed around us again.

What's most sadistic is
There's a term called traumatic memory.
So it's very possible you touched me too.

That fateful night you pasted your sickness
On all of our psyches.
Either way damage done.
Maybe life, or a prison,
Has taken care of you by now.
So I have nothing more to say to you.
I just hope no one else has a story,
About you, where it starts with,
I was just watching TV.

I Love You

Parents' affection? No yearn.
Relatives' connection? No urge.
Even platonic friends? Just there.
Search for a mate? BOOM! Dive deep.

Self-worth hung on tightropes
Of each word spoken
Each face made, each hug given
From a woman.

Without much game,
20s were barren. Good.
Insecurity stifles lust
Buries love in its dark pits.

Self-love, self-care
Came with my 30s.
As did a new sense of
Self, dating, and family.

As a child I was...
Heard? Nope, just seen.
Loved? Nope, just tolerated.
Family? Nope, just told so.

I was all of these things
Unable to show it, they
Had their own demons to fight.
Much as I do mine now.

We've since patched things up
Living peacefully, ghosts
Dissolving in the winds of
Connection and awareness.

Maybe they didn't know
How to say "I love you"
To themselves much like
I'm learning to do to me.

Breaking so many
Generational curses
With each "I love you"
to myself at a time.

Rockstar

Lived life modestly
Just outside the city
But there was more than
What meets the best eye
Survived deep neglect
Sexual abuse
Crippling self-esteem
Single parent house
But I made it out
Alive, prospering

Tonight I'm a rock star

Only five lovers in my life
Actually proud of that
Got to heal without
Hurting many mates
Didn't fall for racism
Or any isms.
Dummy friends who
Abuse, ignore, cut down,
no time for them
Can't sell my morals.

Tonight I'm a rock star

Any of you who
Survived similar lives
Get to stand up, clap,
And back pat yourselves
Be proud of you and your fight.

We're all rock stars tonight

Slurs?

The fuck these people
Come up with slurs
And they ain't even offensive?
Like you gonna call me woke?
Yeah, I'm awake. I can breathe.
I'm socially aware, unlike you.
Like you call me a snowflake?
Snowflakes are beautiful
And each one unique,
Sparkling land each winter.
You gonna call me a cuck?
Showing support for a woman
Isn't being a cuck
You fucking moron.

You fling these insults
Thinking you're hurting us
But it's really like a boomerang
Missing the mark, curving,
And pinging back at you
letting you absorb all the hate
You think you spew unto others.
You're only insulting yourself.
So I'll stop myself at moron.

Dreams

A man: street artist,
Paper, oils, murals his dreams.
A woman: street baller,
W not in her NBA fantasy
A child: full gamer,
Fortnite + Call of Duty,
In his dream, an Esport king.

The man never left the streets.
The woman, bum knee, retired to factories.
The child, turned to drugs, sold his games.

Dreams are just dreams, not reality.
But if you keep them inside
You can still leave parts of them
Along the way in your life.
You lose hope, you lose your dreams and
All the little, pretty pieces giving life worth.

Man's art gives smiles, home roads hang his work.
Woman's school number retired, coaches kids now.
Child cleaned up, cleans up others counseling.

Dreams never fully became reality,
But they kept hope, leaving the
pretty, little parts all over their lives.

Last Kiss

I saw you glistening
that radiant smile
most don't get to see.

We were singing along
to our most loved heavy songs
we're both metal heads.

There was a twinkle in your eye
sitting in my passenger seat
as I drove reasonable speeds.

Endpoint didn't matter much
on this warm summer afternoon,
you and I hand, in hand.

Just the two of us freeing
from the burdens of everyday life
our lives, as chaotic as they were.

You told me to stop the car
near an abandoned bus shelter.
A July day's full light lowering.

We peeked for voyeurs,
slid beneath the roof,
pulled a random curtain down.
Behind it, the spooning began.

Could this be more perfect?
Ensconced in nature,
unkempt, weed-filled field behind us,
we're cuddled, huddled with one another
enjoying each other's company.
I remember when
you first typed my digits
into your phone.
I remember when
we first kissed.
I remember when
you said you saw
forever in my eyes.

All these moments seemed to collide
as we faced each other
and planted even deeper kisses
on our eager, caressing lips.
I could just feel your body sliding gently
loosening with mine while clinging together.
Even more so as our clothing, piece by piece
ended up on the graffiti-filled ground below.
It felt as if our souls were
ping ponging together
like in a crock pot,
simmering in juices,
adding flavor to lives
we didn't know
needed it.

Blurring to a spin,
        I stop, nearing nausea.
        I check, as you turn silent.
This broken apparatus around us sits,
cracked, barren, rusty, resonant.
Feels less homely, almost ghostly.
While waiting for your next move,
I reach into empty air grown cold,
as fall of two kinds set in.
I can't hear your soft moans
or the faint scrunch of us
slowly gyrating, touching the peeling paint
of the walls, this was all I ever had.
The expanse of my dreams is crumbling.
Reality finally sets in deep enough
to kick the denial out of my soul.

Deep breaths followed,
in then out, in then out.
My energy, the love,
the lust, the loss,
the pain, the anger,
the loathing, pours out
like from a tall raincloud,
as I scream violently into the twilight.
Darkening above as the sky holds my tears.
I absorb then shed them out of grief,
shedding the guise that our love was real.

I'll keep crying, until the
last drop rings out my ducts
and drains the pain out of me.
Or else I might as well
keep dreaming.

Moving Picture Recipe

Ingredients
- sweltering humidity
- a storm cloud
- a dash of grey
- 8-9 sun rays
- lawless use of a cellphone
- cop-free highway
- a speeding driver

This recipe can be dangerous to execute.
It should be handled with the utmost care.
You must partner with the sky on this one.

1. The sky above you must destabilize the air with sweltering humidity. This will aid in the growth of storm clouds.

2. Next, the sky must pick a storm cloud not too big yet, and throw in a dash of grey.

3. Now, take the sun and stir down the sun rays into the cloud. The openings will give the rays space to drop through.

4. Place one speeding driver below the scene. Preferably, this would be you.

5. Make sure there's open highway pinched on the sides. Other vehicles could cause accidents or obstructions of view.

6. Then, check for cops. The new "don't look down at your phone" law could be enforced. Plus, fuck the police.

7. Finally, sprinkle in a lawless use of a cellphone and snap a picture of the moment.

When you have finished, analyze the snapshot you took. If it's blurry or with obstructions, repeat instructions from the beginning at a later date and time. Most likely the view has passed for now.

Seasons

I fucking hate you!
Well I fucking hate you too!
A night argument over bullshit
but really more an unmasking
as our pain unleashed,
betroths with a storm of sound.
We feel ourselves empty
and weaken, and crumble
like when springs tornadoes
snap and break all in sight,
rip all to shreds, blow it away.
I know I have time to grow,
but can we do so together?

After morning walk with my son
and terrier, dog causally
trotting, bathing in
the strengthening sun.
My son stops to observe
insects dancing, bang on poles,
make music and gallop back
to catch up to me, to us.
Gratefulness isn't clearly visible
through extreme pain.
Summer heat isn't always hot.
It might give you a crisp breeze
reminding you of life's beauty.

We're rekindling, sparking a flame
amidst the campfire, just us.
No kids, no pets, alone with nature,
two lovers lusting, yearning again.
But when night falls to morning
I notice she's the same woman
who I shared screams with,
shared so much pain, so many
scars that can't heal.
Like Autumn leaves turning orange,
so radiant for a few weeks,
they eventually fall, wither, brown,
and crunch to dust.

As I pack my bags, and say goodbyes
know we still have our son, our pet,
our own lives, and make wishes for all
scattering the ashes of the good remains
of what we once had, and the lessons
learned. we can let them brown like
when snow covers grass, freezing it,
letting it absorb the nutrients of water.
When our unromantic winter ends,
we'll return to the warming of spring
with many more nutrients
to enrich the lives of all around.

Make patchwork of your seasons,
as they come and they go.
You'll be prouder of yourself
the bigger it becomes,
the more colors you see,
the more senses you feel,
the more you learn
from the tattered pieces.

Glass

Staring at the reflection,
in thick air, feeling tension
turn nerves to livewires,
a pained face with a
cracked, dirty grin
dulls the glimmer
of the clean glass,
A sign on the top of it reads.
DON'T TAP THE GLASS

Was he looking at a fish tank?
There were no fish,
no running water,
no flush of the machines
keeping it all flowing.
Curiosity killed the cat
and could hurt a fish.
Initially, paralyzed with worry
And empty from lost will,
He now inched fingers close,
Stirring, trembling, forward.

He tapped, once, twice,
and wondered if he'd see
a tail, scales, maybe a cat.
Third, a bit stronger,
he heard the shake,
Fourth time, loud and hardest,
SPLASH! CRASH!
the glass shatters onto
the floor, the noise
bouncing off white walls cornering,
bending them nearly.
What he saw, seemed alien
to him, yet, all too familiar.

Remnants of every bastard trauma
each shard flashing a story
Of fending off molesters
Or hiding from school bullies
Or hearing mom's drunken words
Seeing her drunken actions.

Of the emotional neglect of a
Family who said "just push thru it".

Of his freezing fear of women
And the rejection past "lovers" brought.
Of his own mental shackles
Telling himself he was worthy of no good.
Of all of the days of inaction
Against his own demons,
Each damn trauma lies in the pieces
Shattered all over the floor.

His reflection gone,
he felt his grin smoothed
unforced like the air now swaying,
massaging, thinning,
a soothing energy, light
as when pierced by foreign light,
the glass slivers become kaleidoscopes
the lessons learned and
the strength forged,
turned the achromatic matter
into rainbows of colors.
Through pressure, like a diamond,
Thru darkness, like a luminescent fish
only the sun brought out the light,
Or maybe light speared through the dark.

He learned he can make art
with his darkness, or his dullness.
His terror. His pain. His emptiness.
A lesson that could be
put to practice more than once.
He might have to tap the glass again.
Maybe it was meant to break.

Don't Tap It

DON'T TAP THE GLASS
Onlookers watching with rising wonder
Handlers scanning for any malcontents
Loved ones cover faces with trembling hands.

DON'T TAP THE GLASS
One from a seat above the glass said flatly.
One frantic man, swimming like a fish
In open air, dancing wildly for food.

PLEASE DON'T TAP THE GLASS
Officer above keeps reminding
As viewers keep disobeying that request
While the fish keeps gyrating.

PLEASE STAY DOWN, DON'T CLIMB
Unlike a fish, the human tries to climb the glass
Slip, slide, fall, a few hard thumps
Motivate him to stop, stare straight.

DON'T TAP THE GLASS
The fish runs head on, full speed at the front wall.
Patrons run for safety as the fish gathers speed.
He lunges forward into the glass, HARD.

To his dismay, as he tumbles onto the grass,
He looks down then back, no shards, no cuts,
No four walls, no handlers, no fans, no taps.
Just his mom telling his brother to stop tapping
The goldfish bowl.

About the author:

Manny Cartagena is a budding poet from idyllic Berks County. Manny has been published in PA Bards' Eastern PA Poetry Review, Worlds of Possibility, Queens Quarterly, and New Plains Review. He has been a constant in the Southeastern PA literary scene for the last year and has been writing for over 15 years. His love of nature and intense capacity for uncomfortable emotions combine and spill onto the pages of his work, including Valley Therapy.

www.ingramcontent.com/pod-product-compliance
Lightning Source LLC
LaVergne TN
LVHW050948080826
845145LV00004B/1451

* 9 7 8 1 9 5 2 3 5 2 3 0 0 *